Reflections on War and Death

&

On Aphasia

(2 Books)

SIGMUND FREUD

2017 by McAllister Editions (MCALLISTEREDITIONS@GMAIL.COM). This book is a classic, and a product of its time. It does not reflect the same views on race, gender, sexuality, ethnicity, and interpersonal relations as it would if it was written today.

CONTENTS

BOOK ONE 1
REFLECTIONS ON WAR AND DEATH 1
  I. THE DISAPPOINTMENTS OF WAR 1
  II. OUR ATTITUDE TOWARDS DEATH 32
BOOK TWO. ON APHASIA 59
  INTRODUCTION 59
  CLINICAL STUDIES OF THE UNILATERAL CEREBRAL PALSIES OF CHILDREN. . 63
  A CASE OF SUCCESSFUL TREATMENT BY HYPNOTISM WITH SOME REMARKS ON THE ORIGIN OF HYSTERICAL SYMPTOMS THROUGH "COUNTER WILL". 66
  ON THE PSYCHICAL MECHANISM OF HYSTERICAL PHENOMENA. 69
  AN ACCOUNT OF THE CEREBRAL DIPLEGIAS OF CHILDHOOD (IN CONNECTION WITH LITTLE'S DISEASE.) 72
  ON FAMILIAL FORMS OF CEREBRAL DIPLEGIAS. 79
  THE CEREBRAL DIPLEGIAS OF CHILDREN. 81
  THE NEURO-PSYCHOSES OF DEFENSE: 84
  OBSESSIONS AND PHOBIAS: 87

•

BOOK ONE
REFLECTIONS ON WAR AND DEATH

I. The Disappointments of War

CAUGHT in the whirlwind of these war times, without any real information or any perspective upon the great changes that have already occurred or are about to be enacted, lacking all premonition of the future, it is small wonder that we ourselves become confused as to the meaning of impressions which crowd in upon us or of the value of the judgments we are forming. It would seem as though no event had ever destroyed so much of the precious heritage of mankind, confused so many of the clearest intellects or so thoroughly debased what is highest.

Even science has lost her dispassionate impartiality. Her deeply embittered votaries are intent upon seizing her weapons to do their share in the battle against the enemy. The anthropologist has to declare his opponent inferior and degenerate, the psychiatrist must diagnose him as mentally deranged. Yet it is probable that we are affected out of all proportion by the evils of these times and have no right to compare them with the evils of other times through which we have not lived.

The individual who is not himself a combatant and therefore has not become a cog in the gigantic war machinery, feels confused in his bearings and hampered in his activities. I think any little suggestion that will make it easier for him to see his way more clearly will be welcome. Among the factors which cause the stay-at-home so much spiritual misery and are so hard to endure there are two in particular which I should like to emphasize and discuss. I mean the disappointment that this war has called forth and the altered attitude towards death to which it, in common with other wars, forces us.

When I speak of disappointment everybody knows at once what I mean. One need not be a sentimentalist, one may realize the biological and physiological necessity of suffering in the economy of human life, and yet one may condemn the methods and the aims of war and long for its termination. To be sure, we used to say that wars cannot cease as long as nations live under such varied conditions, as long as they place such different values upon the individual life, and as long as the animosities which divide them represent such powerful psychic forces. We were therefore quite ready to believe that for some time to come there would be wars between primitive and civilized nations and between those divided by color, as well as with and among the partly enlightened and more or less civilized peoples of Europe. But we dared to hope differently. We expected that the great ruling nations of the white race, the leaders of mankind, who had cultivated world wide interests, and to whom we owe the technical progress in the control of nature as well as the creation of artistic and scientific cultural standards— we expected that these nations would find some other way of settling their differences and conflicting interests.

Each of these nations had set a high moral standard to which the individual had to conform if he wished to be a member of the civilized community.

These frequently over strict precepts demanded a great deal of him, a great self-restraint and a marked renunciation of his impulses. Above all he was forbidden to resort to lying and cheating, which are so extraordinarily useful in competition with others. The civilized state considered these moral standards the foundation of its existence, it drastically interfered if anyone dared to question them and often declared it improper even to submit them to the test of intellectual criticism. It was therefore assumed that the state itself would respect them and would do nothing that might contradict the foundations of its own existence. To be sure, one was aware that scattered among these civilized nations there were certain remnants of races that were quite universally disliked, and were therefore reluctantly and only to a certain extent permitted to participate in the common work of civilization where they had proved themselves sufficiently fit for the task. But the great nations themselves, one should have thought, had acquired sufficient understanding for the qualities they had in common and enough tolerance for their differences so that, unlike in the days of classical antiquity, the words "foreign" and "hostile" should no longer be synonyms.

Trusting to this unity of civilized races countless people left hearth and home to live in strange lands and trusted their fortunes to the friendly relations existing between the various countries. And even he who was not tied down to the same spot by the exigencies of life could combine all the advantages and charms of civilized countries into a newer and greater fatherland which he could enjoy without hindrance or suspicion. He thus took delight in the blue and the grey ocean, the beauty of snow clad mountains and of the green lowlands, the magic of the north woods and the grandeur of southern vegetation, the atmosphere of landscapes upon which great historical memories rest, and the peace of untouched nature. The new fatherland was to him also a museum, filled with the treasure that all the artists of the world for many centuries had created and left behind. While he wandered from one hall to another in this museum he could give his impartial appreciation to the varied types of perfection that had been developed among his distant compatriots by the mixture of blood, by history, and by the peculiarities of physical environment. Here cool, inflexible energy was developed to the highest degree, there the graceful art of beautifying life, elsewhere the sense of law and order, or other qualities that have made man master of the earth.

We must not forget that every civilized citizen of the world had created his own special "Parnassus" and his own "School of Athens." Among the great philosophers, poets, and artists of all nations he had selected those to whom he considered himself indebted for the best enjoyment and understanding of life, and he associated them in his homage both with the immortal ancients and with the familiar masters of his own tongue. Not one of these great figures seemed alien to him just because he spoke in a different language; be it the incomparable explorer of human passions or the intoxicated worshiper of beauty, the mighty and threatening seer or the sensitive scoffer, and yet he never reproached himself with having become an apostate to his own nation and his beloved mother tongue.

The enjoyment of this common civilization was occasionally disturbed by voices which warned that in consequence of traditional differences wars were unavoidable even between those who shared this civilization. One did not want to believe this, but what did one imagine such a war to be like if it should ever come about? No doubt it was to be an opportunity to show the progress in man's community feeling since the days when the Greek amphictyonies had forbidden the destruction of a city belonging to the league, the felling of her oil trees and the cutting off of her water supply. It would be a chivalrous bout of arms for the sole purpose of establishing the superiority of one side or the other with the greatest possible avoidance of severe suffering which could contribute nothing to the decision, with complete protection for the wounded, who must withdraw from the battle, and for the physicians and nurses who devote themselves to their care. With every consideration, of course, for noncombatants, for the women who are removed from the activities of war, and for the children who, when grown up, are to become friends and co-workers on both sides. And with the maintenance, finally, of all the international projects and institutions in which the civilized community of peace times had expressed its corporate life.

Such a war would still be horrible enough and full of burdens, but it would not have interrupted the development of ethical relations between the large human units, between nations and states.

But the war in which we did not want to believe broke out and brought—disappointment. It is not only bloodier and more destructive than any foregoing war, as a result of the tremendous development of weapons of attack and defense, but it is at least as cruel, bitter, and merciless as any earlier war. It places itself above all the restrictions pledged in times of peace, the so-called rights of nations, it does not acknowledge the prerogatives of the wounded and of physicians, the distinction between peaceful and fighting members of the population, or the claims of private property. It hurls down in blind rage whatever bars its way, as though there were to be no future and no peace after it is over.

It tears asunder all community bonds among the struggling peoples and threatens to leave a bitterness which will make impossible any re-establishment of these ties for a long time to come.

It has also brought to light the barely conceivable phenomenon of civilized nations knowing and understanding each other so little that one can turn from the other with hate and loathing. Indeed one of these great civilized nations has become so universally disliked that it is even attempted to cast it out from the civilized community as though it were barbaric, although this very nation has long proved its eligibility through contribution after contribution of brilliant achievements. We live in the hope that impartial history will furnish the proof that this very nation, in whose language I am writing and for whose victory our dear ones are fighting, has sinned least against the laws of human civilization. But who is privileged to step forward at such a time as judge in his own defense?

Races are roughly represented by the states they form and these states by the governments which guide them. The individual citizen can prove with dismay in this war what occasionally thrust itself upon him already in times of peace, namely, that the state forbids him to do wrong not because it wishes to do away with wrongdoing but because it wishes to monopolize it, like salt and tobacco. A state at war makes free use of every injustice, every act of violence, that would dishonor the individual. It employs not only permissible cunning but conscious lies and intentional deception against the enemy, and this to a degree which apparently outdoes what was customary in previous wars. The state demands the utmost obedience and sacrifice of its citizens, but at the same time it treats them as children through an excess of secrecy and a censorship of news and expression of opinion which render the minds of those who are thus intellectually repressed defenseless against every unfavorable situation and every wild rumor. It absolves itself from guarantees and treaties by which it was bound to other states, makes unabashed confession of its greed and aspiration to power, which the individual is then supposed to sanction out of patriotism.

Let the reader not object that the state cannot abstain from the use of injustice because it would thereby put itself at a disadvantage. For the individual, too, obedience to moral standards and abstinence from brutal acts of violence are as a rule very disadvantageous, and the state but rarely proves itself capable of indemnifying the individual for the sacrifice it demands of him. Nor is it to be wondered at that the loosening of moral ties between the large human units has had a pronounced effect upon the morality of the individual, for our conscience is not the inexorable judge that teachers of ethics say it is; it has its origin in nothing but "social fear." Wherever the community suspends its reproach the suppression of evil desire also ceases, and men commit acts of cruelty, treachery, deception, and brutality, the very possibility of which would have been considered incompatible with their level of culture.

Thus the civilized world-citizen of whom I spoke before may find himself helpless in a world that has grown strange to him when he sees his great fatherland disintegrated, the possessions common to mankind destroyed, and his fellow citizens divided and debased.

Nevertheless several things might be said in criticism of his disappointment. Strictly speaking it is not justified, for it consists in the destruction of an illusion. Illusions commend themselves to us because they save us pain and allow us to enjoy pleasure instead. We must therefore accept it without complaint when they sometimes collide with a bit of reality against which they are dashed to pieces.

Two things have roused our disappointment in this war: the feeble morality of states in their external relations which have inwardly acted as guardians of moral standards, and the brutal behavior of individuals of the highest culture of whom one would not have believed any such thing possible.

Let us begin with the second point and try to sum up the view which we wish to criticise in a single compact statement. Through what process does the individual reach a higher stage of morality? The first answer will probably be: He is really good and noble from birth, in the first place. It is hardly necessary to give this any further consideration. The second answer will follow the suggestion that a process of development is involved here and will probably assume that this development consists in eradicating the evil inclinations of man and substituting good inclinations under the influence of education and cultural environment. In that case we may indeed wonder that evil should appear again so actively in persons who have been educated in this way.

But this answer also contains the theory which we wish to contradict. In reality there is no such thing as "eradicating" evil. Psychological, or strictly speaking, psychoanalytic investigation proves, on the contrary, that the deepest character of man consists of impulses of an elemental kind which are similar in all human beings, the aim of which is the gratification of certain primitive needs. These impulses are in themselves neither good or evil. We classify them and their manifestations according to their relation to the needs and demands of the human community. It is conceded that all the impulses which society rejects as evil, such as selfishness and cruelty, are of this primitive nature.

These primitive impulses go through a long process of development before they can become active in the adult. They become inhibited and diverted to other aims and fields, they unite with each other, change their objects and in part turn against one's own person. The formation of reactions against certain impulses give the deceptive appearance of a change of content, as if egotism had become altruism and cruelty had changed into sympathy. The formation of these reactions is favored by the fact that many impulses appear almost from the beginning in contrasting pairs; this is a remarkable state of affairs called the ambivalence of feeling and is quite unknown to the layman. This feeling is best observed and grasped through the fact that intense love and intense hate occur so frequently in the same person. Psychoanalysis goes further and states that the two contrasting feelings not infrequently take the same person as their object.

What we call the character of a person does not really emerge until the fate of all these impulses has been settled, and character, as we all know, is very inadequately defined in terms of either "good" or "evil." Man is seldom entirely good or evil, he is "good" on the whole in one respect and "evil" in another, or "good" under certain conditions, and decidedly "evil" under others. It is interesting to learn that the earlier infantile existence of intense "bad" impulses is often the necessary condition of being "good" in later life. The most pronounced childish egotists may become the most helpful and self-sacrificing citizens; the majority of idealists, humanitarians, and protectors of animals have developed from little sadists and animal tormentors.

The transformation of "evil" impulses is the result of two factors operating in the same sense, one inwardly and the other outwardly. The inner factor consists in influencing the evil or selfish impulses through erotic elements, the love needs of man interpreted in the widest sense. The addition of erotic components transforms selfish impulses into social impulses. We learn to value being loved as an advantage for the sake of which we can renounce other advantages. The outer factor is the force of education which represents the demands of the civilized environment and which is then continued through the direct influence of the cultural *milieu*.

Civilization is based upon the renunciation of impulse gratification and in turn demands the same renunciation of impulses from every newcomer. During the individual's life a constant change takes place from outer to inner compulsion. The influences of civilization work through the erotic components to bring about the transformation of more and more of the selfish tendencies into altruistic and social tendencies. We may indeed assume that the inner compulsion which makes itself felt in the development of man was originally, that is, in the history of mankind, a purely external compulsion. Today people bring along a certain tendency (disposition) to transform the egotistic into social impulses as a part of their hereditary organization, which then responds to further slight incentives to complete the transformation. A part of this transformation of impulse must also be made during life. In this way the individual man is not only under the influence of his own contemporary cultural *milieu* but is also subject to the influences of his ancestral civilization.

If we call a person's individual capacity for transforming his egotistical impulses under the influence of love his cultural adaptability, we can say that this consists of two parts, one congenital and the other acquired, and we may add that the relation of these two to each other and to the untransformed part of the emotional life is a very variable one.

In general we are inclined to rate the congenital part too highly, and are also in danger of over-valuing the whole cultural adaptability in its relation to that part of the impulse life which has remained primitive, that is, we are misled into judging people to be "better" than they really are. For there is another factor which clouds our judgment and falsifies the result in favor of what we are judging.

We are of course in no position to observe the impulses of another person. We deduce them from his actions and his conduct, which we trace back to motives springing from his emotional life. In a number of cases such a conclusion is necessarily incorrect. The same actions which are "good" in the civilized sense may sometimes originate in "noble" motives and sometimes not. Students of the theory of ethics call only those acts "good" which are the expression of good impulses and refuse to acknowledge others as such. But society is on the whole guided by practical aims and does not bother about this distinction; it is satisfied if a man adapts his conduct and his actions to the precepts of civilization and asks little about his motives.

We have heard that the outer compulsion which education and environment exercise upon a man brings about a further transformation of his impulse life for the good, the change from egotism to altruism. But this is not the necessary or regular effect of the outer compulsion. Education and environment have not only love premiums to offer but work with profit premiums of another sort, namely rewards and punishments. They can therefore bring it about that a person subject to their influence decides in favor of good conduct in the civilized sense without any ennobling of impulse or change from egotistic into altruistic inclinations. On the whole the consequence remains the same; only special circumstances will reveal whether the one person is always good because his impulses compel him to be so while another person is good only in so far as this civilized behavior is of advantage to his selfish purposes. But our superficial knowledge of the individual gives us no means of distinguishing the two cases, and we shall certainly be misled by our optimism into greatly over-estimating the number of people who have been transformed by civilization.

Civilized society, which demands good conduct and does not bother about the impulse on which it is based, has thus won over a great many people to civilized obedience who do not thereby follow their own natures. Encouraged by this success, society has permitted itself to be misled into putting the ethical demands as high as possible, thereby forcing its members to move still further from their emotional dispositions. A continual emotional suppression is imposed upon them, the strain of which is indicated by the appearance of the most remarkable reactions and compensations.

In the field of sexuality, where such suppression is most difficult to carry out, it results in reactions known as neurotic ailments. In other fields the pressure of civilization shows no pathological results but manifests itself in distorted characters and in the constant readiness of the inhibited impulses to enforce their gratification at any fitting opportunity.

Anyone thus forced to react continually to precepts that are not the expressions of his impulses lives, psychologically speaking, above his means, and may be objectively described as a hypocrite, whether he is clearly conscious of this difference or not. It is undeniable that our contemporary civilization favors this sort of hypocrisy to an extraordinary extent. One might even venture to assert that it is built upon such a hypocrisy and would have to undergo extensive changes if man were to undertake to live according to the psychological truth. There are therefore more civilized hypocrites than truly cultured persons, and one can even discuss the question whether a certain amount of civilized hypocrisy is not indispensable to maintain civilization because the already organized cultural adaptability of the man of today would perhaps not suffice for the task of living according to the truth. On the other hand the maintenance of civilization even on such questionable grounds offers the prospect that with every new generation a more extensive transformation of impulses will pave the way for a better civilization.

These discussions have already afforded us the consolation that our mortification and painful disappointment on account of the uncivilized behavior of our fellow world citizens in this war were not justified. They rested upon an illusion to which we had succumbed. In reality they have not sunk as deeply as we feared because they never really rose as high as we had believed. The fact that states and races abolished their mutual ethical restrictions not unnaturally incited them to withdraw for a time from the existing pressure of civilization and to sanction a passing gratification of their suppressed impulses. In doing so their relative morality within their own national life probably suffered no rupture.

But we can still further deepen our understanding of the change which this war has brought about in our former compatriots and at the same time take warning not to be unjust to them. For psychic evolution shows a peculiarity which is not found in any other process of development. When a town becomes a city or a child grows into a man, town and child disappear in the city and in the man. Only memory can sketch in the old features in the new picture; in reality the old materials and forms have been replaced by new ones. It is different in the case of psychic evolution. One can describe this unique state of affairs only by saying that every previous stage of development is preserved next to the following one from which it has evolved; the succession stipulates a co-existence although the material in which the whole series of changes has taken place remains the same.

The earlier psychic state may not have manifested itself for years but nevertheless continues to exist to the extent that it may some day again become the form in which psychic forces express themselves, in fact the only form, as though all subsequent developments had been annulled and made regressive. This extraordinary plasticity of psychic development is not without limits as to its direction; one can describe it as a special capacity for retrograde action or regression, for it sometimes happens that a later and higher stage of development that has been abandoned cannot be attained again. But the primitive conditions can always be reconstructed; the primitive psyche is in the strictest sense indestructible.

The so-called mental diseases must make the impression on the layman of mental and psychic life fallen into decay. In reality the destruction concerns only later acquisitions and developments. The nature of mental diseases consists in the return to former states of the affective life and function. An excellent example of the plasticity of the psychic life is the state of sleep, which we all court every night.

Since we know how to interpret even the maddest and most confused dreams, we know that every time we go to sleep we throw aside our hard won morality like a garment in order to put it on again in the morning. This laying bare is, of course, harmless, because we are paralyzed and condemned to inactivity by the sleeping state.

Only the dream can inform us of the regression of our emotional life to an earlier stage of development. Thus, for instance, it is worthy of note that all our dreams are governed by purely egotistic motives. One of my English friends once presented this theory to a scientific meeting in America, whereupon a lady present made the remark that this might perhaps be true of Austrians, but she ventured to assert for herself and her friends that even in dreams they always felt altruistically. My friend, although himself a member of the English race, was obliged to contradict the lady energetically on the basis of his experience in dream analysis. The noble Americans are just as egotistic in their dreams as the Austrians.

The transformation of impulses upon which our cultural adaptibility rests can therefore also be permanently or temporarily made regressive. Without doubt the influences of war belong to those forces which can create such regressions; we therefore need not deny cultural adaptibility to all those who at present are acting in such an uncivilized manner, and may expect that the refinement of their impulses will continue in more peaceful times.

But there is perhaps another symptom of our fellow citizens of the world which has caused us no less surprise and fear than this descent from former ethical heights which has been so painful to us. I mean the lack of insight that our greatest intellectual leaders have shown, their obduracy, their inaccessibility to the most impressive arguments, their uncritical credulity concerning the most contestable assertions. This certainly presents a sad picture, and I wish expressly to emphasize that I am by no means a blinded partisan who finds all the intellectual mistakes on one side. But this phenomenon is more easily explained and far less serious than the one which we have just considered. Students of human nature and philosophers have long ago taught us that we do wrong to value our intelligence as an independent force and to overlook its dependence upon our emotional life. According to their view our intellect can work reliably only when it is removed from the influence of powerful incitements; otherwise it acts simply as an instrument at the beck and call of our will and delivers the results which the will demands. Logical argumentation is therefore powerless against affective interests; that is why arguing with reasons which, according to Falstaff, are as common as blackberries, are so fruitless where our interests are concerned. Whenever possible psychoanalytic experience has driven home this assertion. It is in a position to prove every day that the cleverest people suddenly behave as unintelligently as defectives as soon as their understanding encounters emotional resistance, but that they regain their intelligence completely as soon as this resistance has been overcome. This blindness to logic which this war has so frequently conjured up in just our best fellow citizens, is therefore a secondary phenomenon, the result of emotional excitement and destined, we hope, to disappear simultaneously with it.

If we have thus come to a fresh understanding of our estranged fellow citizens we can more easily bear the disappointment which nations have caused us, for of them we must only make demands of a far more modest nature. They are perhaps repeating the development of the individual and at the present day still exhibit very primitive stages of development with a correspondingly slow progress towards the formation of higher unities. It is in keeping with this that the educational factor of an outer compulsion to morality, which we found so active in the individual, is barely perceptible in them. We had indeed hoped that the wonderful community of interests established by intercourse and the exchange of products would result in the beginning of such a compulsion, but it seems that nations obey their passions of the moment far more than their interests. At most they make use of their interests to justify the gratification of their passions.

It is indeed a mystery why the individual members of nations should disdain, hate, and abhor each other at all, even in times of peace. I do not know why it is. It seems as if all the moral achievements of the individual were obliterated in the case of a large number of people, not to mention millions, until only the most primitive, oldest, and most brutal psychic inhibitions remained.

Perhaps only later developments will succeed in changing these lamentable conditions. But a little more truthfulness and straightforward dealing on all sides, both in the relation of people towards each other and between themselves and those who govern them, might smooth the way for such a change.

II. Our Attitude Towards Death

IT remains for us to consider the second factor of which I have already spoken which accounts for our feeling of strangeness in a world which used to seem so beautiful and familiar to us. I refer to the disturbance in our former attitude towards death.

Our attitude had not been a sincere one. To listen to us we were, of course, prepared to maintain that death is the necessary termination of life, that everyone of us owes nature his death and must be prepared to pay his debt, in short, that death was natural, undeniable, and inevitable. In practice we were accustomed to act as if matters were quite different. We have shown an unmistakable tendency to put death aside, to eliminate it from life. We attempted to hush it up, in fact, we have the proverb: to think of something as of death. Of course we meant our own death. We cannot, indeed, imagine our own death;

whenever we try to do so we find that we survive ourselves as spectators. The school of psychoanalysis could thus assert that at bottom no one believes in his own death, which amounts to saying: in the unconscious every one of us is convinced of his immortality.

As far as the death of another person is concerned every man of culture will studiously avoid mentioning this possibility in the presence of the person in question. Only children ignore this restraint; they boldly threaten each other with the possibility of death, and are quite capable of giving expression to the thought of death in relation to the persons they love, as, for instance: Dear Mama, when unfortunately, you are dead, I shall do so and so. The civilized adult also likes to avoid entertaining the thought of another's death lest he seem harsh or unkind, unless his profession as a physician or a lawyer brings up the question. Least of all would he permit himself to think of somebody's death if this event is connected with a gain of freedom, wealth, or position. Death is, of course, not deferred through our sensitiveness on the subject, and when it occurs we are always deeply affected, as if our expectations had been shattered. We regularly lay stress upon the unexpected causes of death, we speak of the accident, the infection, or advanced age, and thus betray our endeavor to debase death from a necessity to an accident. A large number of deaths seems unspeakably dreadful to us. We assume a special attitude towards the dead, something almost like admiration for one who has accomplished a very difficult feat. We suspend criticism of him, overlooking whatever wrongs he may have done, and issue the command, *de mortuis nil nisi bene:* we act as if we were justified in singing his praises at the funeral oration, and inscribe only what is to his advantage on the tombstone. This consideration for the dead, which he really no longer needs, is more important to us than the truth and to most of us, certainly, it is more important than consideration for the living.

This conventional attitude of civilized people towards death is made still more striking by our complete collapse at the death of a person closely related to us, such as a parent, a wife or husband, a brother or sister, a child or a dear friend. We bury our hopes, our wishes, and our desires with the dead, we are inconsolable and refuse to replace our loss. We act in this case as if we belonged to the tribe of the Asra who also die when those whom they love perish. [1]

But this attitude of ours towards death exerts a powerful influence upon our lives. Life becomes impoverished and loses its interest when life itself, the highest stake in the game of living, must not be risked. It becomes as hollow and empty as an American flirtation in which it is understood from the beginning that nothing is to happen, in contrast to a continental love affair in which both partners must always bear in mind the serious consequences. Our emotional ties, the unbearable intensity of

---

[1] Compare Heine's poem, "Der Asra," Louis Untermeyer's translation, p. 269, Henry Holt & Co., 1917.

our grief, make us disinclined to court dangers for ourselves and those belonging to us. We do not dare to contemplate a number of undertakings that are dangerous but really indispensable, such as aeroplane flights, expeditions to distant countries, and experiments with explosive substances. We are paralyzed by the thought of who is to replace the son to his mother, the husband to his wife, or the father to his children, should an accident occur. A number of other renunciations and exclusions result from this tendency to rule out death from the calculations of life. And yet the motto of the Hanseatic League said: *Navigare necesse est, vivere non necesse:* It is necessary to sail the seas, but not to live.

It is therefore inevitable that we should seek compensation for the loss of life in the world of fiction, in literature, and in the theater. There we still find people who know how to die, who are even quite capable of killing others. There alone the condition for reconciling ourselves to death is fulfilled, namely, if beneath all the vicissitudes of life a permanent life still remains to us. It is really too sad that it may happen in life as in chess, where a false move can force us to lose the game, but with this difference, that we cannot begin a return match. In the realm of fiction we find the many lives in one for which we crave. We die in identification with a certain hero and yet we outlive him and, quite unharmed, are prepared to die again with the next hero.

It is obvious that the war must brush aside this conventional treatment of death. Death is no longer to be denied; we are compelled to believe in it. People really die and no longer one by one, but in large numbers, often ten thousand in one day. It is no longer an accident. Of course, it still seems accidental whether a particular bullet strikes this man or that but the survivor may easily be struck down by a second bullet, and the accumulation of deaths ends the impression of accident. Life has indeed become interesting again; it has once more received its full significance.

Let us make a division here and separate those who risk their lives in battle from those who remain at home, where they can only expect to lose one of their loved ones through injury, illness, or infection. It would certainly be very interesting to study the changes in the psychology of the combatants but I know too little about this. We must stick to the second group, to which we ourselves belong. I have already stated that I think the confusion and paralysis of our activities from which we are suffering is essentially determined by the fact that we cannot retain our previous attitude towards death. Perhaps it will help us to direct our psychological investigation to two other attitudes towards death, one of which we may ascribe to primitive man, while the other is still preserved, though invisible to our consciousness, in the deeper layers of our psychic life.

The attitude of prehistoric man towards death is, of course, known to us only through deductions and reconstructions, but I am of the opinion that these have given us fairly trustworthy information.

Primitive man maintained a very curious attitude towards death. It is not at all consistent but rather contradictory. On the one hand he took death very seriously, recognized it as the termination of life, and made use of it in this sense; but, on the other hand, he also denied death and reduced it to nothingness. This contradiction was made possible by the fact that he maintained a radically different position in regard to the death of others, a stranger or an enemy, than in regard to his own. The death of another person fitted in with his idea, it signified the annihilation of the hated one, and primitive man had no scruples against bringing it about. He must have been a very passionate being, more cruel and vicious than other animals. He liked to kill and did it as a matter of course. Nor need we attribute to him the instinct which restrains other animals from killing and devouring their own species.

As a matter of fact the primitive history of mankind is filled with murder. The history of the world which is still taught to our children is essentially a series of race murders. The dimly felt sense of guilt under which man has lived since archaic times, and which in many religions has been condensed into the assumption of a primal guilt, a hereditary sin, is probably the expression of a blood guilt, the burden of which primitive man assumed. In my book entitled "Totem and Taboo," 1913, I have followed the hints of W. Robertson Smith, Atkinson, and Charles Darwin in the attempt to fathom the nature of this ancient guilt, and am of the opinion that the Christian doctrine of today still makes it possible for us to work back to its origin. [2]

If the Son of God had to sacrifice his life to absolve mankind from original sin, then, according to the law of retaliation, the return of like for like, this sin must have been an act of killing, a murder. Nothing

---
[2] Totem and Taboo.

else could call for the sacrifice of a life in expiation. And if original sin was a sin against the God Father, the oldest sin of mankind must have been a patricide—the killing of the primal father of the primitive human horde, whose memory picture later was transfigured into a deity. [3]

Primitive man was as incapable of imagining and realizing his own death as any one of us are today. But a case arose in which the two opposite attitudes towards death clashed and came into conflict with each other, with results that are both significant and far reaching. Such a case was given when primitive man saw one of his own relatives die, his wife, child, or friend, whom he certainly loved as we do ours; for love cannot be much younger than the lust for murder. In his pain he must have discovered that he, too, could die, an admission against which his whole being must have revolted, for everyone of these loved ones was a part of his own beloved

---

[3] Totem and Taboo Ch.IV

self. On the other hand again, every such death was satisfactory to him, for there was also something foreign in each one of these persons. The law of emotional ambivalence, which today still governs our emotional relations to those whom we love, certainly obtained far more widely in primitive times. The beloved dead had nevertheless roused some hostile feelings in primitive man just because they had been both friends and enemies.

Philosophers have maintained that the intellectual puzzle which the picture of death presented to primitive man forced him to reflect and became the starting point of every speculation. I believe the philosophers here think too philosophically, they give too little consideration to the primary effective motive. I should therefore like to correct and limit the above assertion; primitive man probably triumphed at the side of the corpse of the slain enemy, without finding any occasion to puzzle his head about the riddle of life and death. It was not the intellectual puzzle or any particular death which roused the spirit of inquiry in man, but the conflict of emotions at the death of beloved and withal foreign and hated persons.

From this emotional conflict psychology arose. Man could no longer keep death away from him, for he had tasted of it in his grief for the deceased, but he did not want to acknowledge it, since he could not imagine himself dead. He therefore formed a compromise and concealed his own death but denied it the significance of destroying life, a distinction for which the death of his enemies had given him no motive. He invented spirits during his contemplation of the corpse of the person he loved, and his consciousness of guilt over the gratification which mingled with his grief brought it about that these first created spirits were transformed into evil demons who were to be feared. The changes wrought by death suggested to him to divide the individual into body and soul, at first several souls, and in this way his train of thought paralleled the disintegration process inaugurated by death. The continued remembrance of the dead became the basis of the assumption of other forms of existence and gave him the idea of a future life after apparent death.

These later forms of existence were at first only vaguely associated appendages to those whom death had cut off, and enjoyed only slight esteem until much later times; they still betrayed a very meagre knowledge. The reply which the soul of Achilles made to Odysseus comes to our mind:

> Erst in the life on the earth, no less than a god we revered thee,
> We the Achaeans; and now in the realm of the dead as a monarch
> Here thou dost rule; then why should death thus grieve thee, Achilles?
> Thus did I speak: forthwith then answering thus he addressed me.

Speak not smoothly of death, I beseech, O famous Odysseus,

Better by far to remain on the earth as the thrall of another,

E'en of a portionless man that hath means right scanty of living,

Rather than reign sole king in the realm of the bodiless phantoms.

Odysseus XI, verse 484–491

Translated by H. B. Coterill.

Heine has rendered this in a forcible and bitter parody:

The smallest living philistine,
At Stuckert on the Neckar
Is much happier than I am,
Son of Pelleus, the dead hero,
Shadowy ruler of the Underworld.

It was much later before religions managed to declare this after-life as the more valuable and perfect and to debase our mortal life to a mere preparation for the life to come. It was then only logical to prolong our existence into the past and to invent former existences, transmigrations of souls, and reincarnations, all with the object of depriving death of its meaning as the termination of life. It was as early as this that the denial of death, which we described as the product of conventional culture, originated.

Contemplation of the corpse of the person loved gave birth not only to the theory of the soul, the belief in immortality, and implanted the deep roots of the human sense of guilt, but it also created the first ethical laws. The first and most important prohibition of the awakening conscience declared: Thou shalt not kill. This arose as a reaction against the gratification of hate for the beloved dead which is concealed behind grief, and was gradually extended to the unloved stranger and finally also to the enemy.

Civilized man no longer feels this way in regard to killing enemies. When the fierce struggle of this war will have reached a decision every victorious warrior will joyfully and without delay return home to his wife and children, undisturbed by thoughts of the enemy he has killed either at close quarters or with weapons operating at a distance.

It is worthy of note that the primitive races which still inhabit the earth and who are certainly closer to primitive man than we, act differently in this respect, or have so acted as long as they did not yet feel the influence of our civilization. The savage, such as the Australian, the Bushman, or the inhabitant of Terra del Fuego, is by no means a remorseless murderer; when he returns home as victor from the war path he is not allowed to enter his village or touch his wife until he has expiated his war murders through lengthy and often painful penances. The explanation for this is, of course, related to his superstition; the savage fears the avenging spirit of the slain. But the spirits of the fallen enemy are nothing but the expression of his evil conscience over his blood guilt; behind this superstition there lies concealed a bit of ethical delicacy of feeling which has been lost to us civilized beings. [4]

Pious souls, who would like to think us removed from contact with what is evil and mean, will surely not fail to draw satisfactory conclusions in regard to the strength of the ethical impulses which have been implanted in us from these early and forcible murder prohibitions. Unfortunately this argument proves even more for the opposite contention.

Such a powerful inhibition can only be directed against an equally strong impulse. What no human being desires to do does not have to be forbidden, it is self-exclusive. The very emphasis of the commandment: Thou

---
[4] Totem and Taboo, Ch.IV

shalt not kill, makes it certain that we are descended from an endlessly long chain of generations of murderers, whose love of murder was in their blood as it is perhaps also in ours. The ethical strivings of mankind, with the strength and significance of which we need not quarrel, are an acquisition of the history of man; they have since become, though unfortunately in very variable quantities, the hereditary possessions of people of today.

Let us now leave primitive man and turn to the unconscious in our psyche. Here we depend entirely upon psychoanalytic investigation, the only method which reaches such depths. The question is what is the attitude of our unconscious towards death. In answer we say that it is almost like that of primitive man. In this respect, as well as in many others, the man of prehistoric times lives on, unchanged, in our conscious.

Our unconscious therefore does not believe in its own death; it acts as though it were immortal. What we call our unconscious, those deepest layers in our psyche which consist of impulses, recognizes no negative or any form of denial and resolves all contradictions, so that it does not acknowledge its own death, to which we can give only a negative content. The idea of death finds absolutely no acceptance in our impulses. This is perhaps the real secret of heroism. The rational basis of heroism is dependent upon the decision that one's own life cannot be worth as much as certain abstract common ideals. But I believe that instinctive or impulsive heroism is much more frequently independent of such motivation and simply defies danger on the assurance which animated Hans, the stone-cutter, a character in Anzengruber, who always said to himself: Nothing can happen to me. Or that motivation only serves to clear away the hesitations which might restrain the corresponding heroic reaction in the unconscious. The fear of death, which controls us more frequently than we are aware, is comparatively secondary and is usually the outcome of the consciousness of guilt.

On the other hand we recognize the death of strangers and of enemies and sentence them to it just as willingly and unhesitatingly as primitive man. Here there is indeed a distinction which becomes decisive in practice. Our unconscious does not carry out the killing, it only thinks and wishes it. But it would be wrong to underestimate the psychic reality so completely in comparison to the practical reality. It is really important and full of serious consequences.

In our unconscious we daily and hourly do away with all those who stand in our way, all those who have insulted or harmed us. The expression: "The devil take him," which so frequently crosses our lips in the form of an ill-humored jest, but by which we really intend to say, "Death take him," is a serious and forceful death wish in our unconscious. Indeed our unconscious murders even for trifles; like the old Athenian law of Draco, it knows no other punishment for crime than death, and this not without a certain consistency, for every injury done to our all-mighty and self-glorifying self is at bottom a *crimen laesae majestatis.*

Thus, if we are to be judged by our unconscious wishes, we ourselves are nothing but a band of murderers, just like primitive man. It is lucky that all wishes do not possess the power which people of primitive times attributed to them.[5] For in the cross fire of mutual maledictions mankind would have perished long ago, not excepting the best and wisest of men as well as the most beautiful and charming women.

As a rule the layman refuses to believe these theories of psychoanalysis. They are rejected as calumnies which can be ignored in the face of the assurances of consciousness, while the few signs through which the unconscious betrays itself to consciousness are cleverly overlooked. It is therefore in place here to point out that

---

[5] Totem and Taboo, Ch. III

many thinkers who could not possibly have been influenced by psychoanalysis have very clearly accused our silent thought of a readiness to ignore the murder prohibition in order to clear away what stands in our path. Instead of quoting many examples I have chosen one which is very famous. In his novel, *Père Goriot,* Balzac refers to a place in the works of J. J. Rousseau where this author asks the reader what he would do if, without leaving Paris and, of course, without being discovered, he could kill an old mandarin in Peking, with great profit to himself, by a mere act of the will. He makes it possible for us to guess that he does not consider the life of this dignitary very secure. "To kill your mandarin" has become proverbial for this secret readiness to kill, even on the part of people of today.

There are also a number of cynical jokes and anecdotes which bear witness to the same effect, such as the remark attributed to the husband: "If one of us dies I shall move to Paris." Such cynical jokes would not be possible if they did not have an unavowed truth to reveal which we cannot admit when it is baldly and seriously stated. It is well known that one may even speak the truth in jest.

A case arises for our consciousness, just as it did for primitive man, in which the two opposite attitudes towards death, one of which acknowledges it as the destroyer of life, while the other denies the reality of death, clash and come into conflict. The case is identical for both, it consists of the death of one of our loved ones, of a parent or a partner in wedlock, of a brother or a sister, of a child or a friend. These persons we love are on the one hand a part of our inner possessions and a constituent of our own selves, but on the other hand they are also in part strangers and even enemies. Except in a few instances, even the tenderest and closest love relations also contain a bit of hostility which can rouse an unconscious death wish. But at the present day this ambivalent conflict no longer results in the development of ethics and soul theories, but in neuroses which also gives us a profound insight into the normal psychic life. Doctors who practice psychoanalysis have frequently had to deal with the symptom of over tender care for the welfare of relatives or with wholly unfounded self reproaches after the death of a beloved person. The study of these cases has left them in no doubt as to the significance of unconscious death wishes.

The layman feels an extraordinary horror at the possibility of such an emotion and takes his aversion to it as a legitimate ground for disbelief in the assertions of psychoanalysis. I think he is wrong there. No debasing of our love life is intended and none such has resulted. It is indeed foreign to our comprehension as well as to our feelings to unite love and hate in this manner, but in so far as nature employs these contrasts she brings it about that love is always kept alive and fresh in order to safeguard it against the hate that is lurking behind it. It may be said that we owe the most beautiful unfolding of our love life to the reaction against this hostile impulse which we feel in our hearts.

Let us sum up what we have said. Our unconscious is just as inaccessible to the conception of our own death, just as much inclined to kill the stranger, and just as divided, or ambivalent towards the persons we love as was primitive man. But how far we are removed from this primitive state in our conventionally civilized attitude towards death!

It is easy to see how war enters into this disunity. War strips off the later deposits of civilization and allows the primitive man in us to reappear. It forces us again to be heroes who cannot believe in their own death, it stamps all strangers as enemies whose death we ought to cause or wish; it counsels us to rise above the death of those whom we love. But war cannot be abolished; as long as the conditions of existence among races are so varied and the repulsions between them are so vehement, there will have to be wars. The question then arises whether we shall be the ones to yield and adapt ourselves to it. Shall we not admit that in our civilized attitude towards death we have again lived psychologically beyond our means? Shall we not turn around and avow the truth? Were it not better to give death the place to which it is entitled both in reality and in our thoughts and to reveal a little more of our unconscious attitude towards death which up to now we have so carefully suppressed? This may not appear a very high achievement and in some respects rather a step backwards, a kind of regression, but at least it has the advantage of taking the truth into account a little more and of making life more bearable again. To bear life remains, after all, the first duty of the living. The illusion becomes worthless if it disturbs us in this.

We remember the old saying:

Si vis pacem, para bellum.
If you wish peace, prepare for war.

The times call for a paraphrase:

Si vis vitam, para mortem.
If you wish life, prepare for death.

BOOK TWO.
ON APHASIA

Introduction

After a firm basis for the understanding of cerebral disturbances of speech had been established by the discovery and definite localization of a motor and a sensory aphasia (Broca and Wernicke), the authorities set about tracing the more subtle symptoms of aphasia as well to factors of localization. In this way they arrived at the hypothesis of a conduction aphasia, with subcortical and transcortical, and motor and sensory forms. This critical study is directed against this view of speech disorders and it seeks to introduce for their explanation functional factors in place of the topographical ones. The forms described as subcortical and transcortical are not to be explained by a particular localization of the lesion but by conditions of reduced capacity for conduction in the apparatus of speech. In fact there are no aphasias caused by subcortical lesion. The justification for distinguishing a central aphasia from a conduction aphasia is also disputed. The speech area of the cortex is seen rather as a continuous region of the cortex inserted between the motor fields of the cortex and those of the optic and auditory nerves--a region within which all communication and association subserving speech function takes place. The so-called speech-centres revealed by the pathology of the brain correspond merely to the corners of this field of speech; they are not distinguished functionally from the interior regions; it is only on account of their position in relation to the contiguous cortical centers that they produce more obvious signs when they become disordered.

The nature of the subject treated here called at many points for a closer investigation of the delimitation between the physiological and the psychological approach. Meynert's and Wernicke's views on the localization of ideas in nervous elements have had to be rejected and Meynert's account of a representation of the body in the cerebral cortex has required revision. Two facts of cerebral anatomy, namely (1) that the masses of fibres entering the spinal cord are constantly diminished on passing upwards, owing to the interposition of grey matter, and (2) that there are no direct paths from the periphery of the body to the cortex - these two facts lead to the conclusion that a really complete representation of the body is present only in the grey matter of the cord (as a projection'), whereas in the cortex the periphery of the body is only represented in less detail through selected fibres arranged according to function.

Clinical Studies of the Unilateral Cerebral Palsies of Children.

(In collaboration with Dr. O. Rie.) (No. III of Beiträge zur Kinderheilkunde edited by Dr. M. Kassowitz.)

A monograph describing this affection, based on studies of material in the First Public Institute for Children's Diseases in Vienna, directed by Kassowitz. In ten sections it deals with (1) the history and literature of the cerebral palsies of children;(2) 35 observations of the authors' own, which are then summarized in tabular form and described individually; (3) the analysis of the individual symptoms of the clinical picture; (4) the pathological anatomy; (5) the relations of cerebral palsy to epilepsy and, (6) to infantile poliomyelitis; (7) differential diagnosis and (8) therapy. Achoreatic paresis' is described by the authors for the first time; it is distinguished by peculiar characteristics in its onset and course, and in it the unilateral paresis is from the beginning represented by hemichorea. There is further an account of the findings of an autopsy (lobar sclerosis as a result of an embolism of the middle cerebral artery) on a woman patient described in the Iconographie de la Saltpêtrière. Emphasis is laid on the close relations between epilepsy and the cerebral palsies of children, in consequence of which some cases of apparent epilepsy might deserve to be described ascerebral palsy without palsy'. In connection with the much discussed question as to the existence of a polioencephalitis acuta, which is supposed to constitute the anatomical basis of unilateral cerebral palsy and to offer a complete analogy with poliomyelitis infantilis, the authors argue against this hypothesis of Strümpell's; but they hold firmly to the expectation that a modified view of poliomyelitis acuta infantilis will allow of its being equated with cerebral palsy on another basis. In the therapeutic section are collected the hitherto published reports on the intervention by brain surgeons directed to the cure of genuine or traumatic epilepsy.

A case of successful treatment by hypnotism with some remarks on the origin of hysterical symptoms through "counter will".

A young woman after the birth of her first child was compelled to give up breastfeeding it owing to a complex of hysterical symptoms (loss of appetite, sleeplessness, pains in her breasts, failure of milk-secretion, agitation). When, after the birth of a second child, these obstacles recurred, deep hypnosis on two occasions, accompanied by countersuggestions, succeeded in removing the obstacles, so that the patient became an excellent nursing mother. The same result was brought about a year later in similar circumstances after two more hypnoses. Some remarks are appended on the fact that it is possible in hysterical patients for distressing antithetic or anxious ideas to be realized which normal people are able to inhibit; several observations of tic are traced back to this mechanism of counterwill.

An obituary of the master of neuropathology who died in 1893 and among whose pupils the present writer numbers himself.

On a symptom which often accompanies enuresis nocturna in children.

In perhaps half the cases of children suffering from enuresis we find a hypertonia of the lower extremities the significance and implications of which are unexplained.

On the psychical mechanism of hysterical phenomena.

(Preliminary communication in collaboration with Dr. J. Breuer.)

The mechanism to which Charcot traced back hystero-traumatic paralyses, and the assumption of which enabled him to provoke them deliberately in hypnotized hysterical patients, can also be made responsible for numerous symptoms of what is described as non-traumatic hysteria. If we put the hysteric under hypnosis and lead his thoughts back to the time at which the symptom in question first appeared, a memory of a psychical trauma (or series of traumas) belonging to that time awakens in him with hallucinatory vividness, the symptom having persisted as a mnemic symbol of the trauma. Thus hysterics suffer mainly from reminiscences. If the traumatic scene which has been arrived at in this way is reproduced vividly, accompanied by a generation of affect, the symptom which has hitherto been obstinately maintained disappears. We must therefore suppose that the forgotten memory has been acting like a foreign body in the mind, with the removal of which the irritating phenomena cease. This discovery, first made by Breuer in 1881, can be made the basis of a therapy of hysterical phenomena which deserves to be described as cathartic.

The memories which are revealed as pathogenic, as the roots of hysterical symptoms, are regularly unconscious to the patient. It seems that by thus remaining unconscious they escape the wearing-away process to which psychical material is normally subject. A wearing-away of this sort is brought about by the method of abreaction. Pathogenic memories avoid being dealt with by abreaction either because the experiences concerned have occurred in special psychical states to which hysterical persons are inherently inclined, or because those experiences have been accompanied by an affect which brings about a special psychical state in hysterical persons. A tendency to a 'splitting of consciousness' is accordingly the basic psychical phenomenon in cases of hysteria.

An Account of the Cerebral Diplegias of Childhood (in Connection with Little's Disease.)

(No. III, New Series, of Beiträge zur Kinderheilkunde edited by Dr. M. Kassowitz.)

A supplement to the Clinical Study of the Unilateral Cerebral Palsies of Children summarized under XX above. The history, pathological anatomy and physiology of the affection are treated here in the same order as in the earlier monograph, and the relevant clinical pictures are illustrated by 53 observations made by the author himself. It was, however, necessary in addition to take into account the range of forms that must be described ascerebral diplegias and to point out their clinical similarity. In face of the differences of opinion that prevail in the literature of these disorders, the author has adopted the standpoint of an earlier authority, Little, and has thus arrived at the erection of four principal types, which are described as general spasticity, paraplegic spasticity, general chorea and bilateral athetosis, and bilateral spastic hemiplegia (spastic diplegia).

General spasticity includes the forms which are usually referred to asLittle's disease'. Paraplegic spasticity is the name given to what was earlier regarded as a spinal affection, tabes spastica infantilis. The spastic diplegias correspond most easily to a doubling of unilateral cerebral palsies, but are characterized by a superfluity of symptoms which finds its explanation in the bilateral nature of the cerebral affection. The justification for including general chorea and bilateral athetosis among these types is provided by numerous characteristics of the clinical picture and by the existence of many mixed and transitional forms which link all these types together.

A discussion follows of the relations of these clinical types to the aetiological factors which are here assumed to be operative and to the insufficient number of post-mortem findings that have been reported. The following conclusions are reached:

Cerebral diplegias can be divided according to their origin into (a) those congenitally determined, (b) those arising at the time of birth and (c) those acquired after birth. But it is extremely rarely that this distinction can be drawn from the clinical peculiarities of the case, and not always possible from the anamnesis. All the aetiological factors of the diplegias are enumerated: prenatal (trauma, illness, or shock affecting the mother, place of the child in the family); operative at the time of birth (the factors stressed by Little, namely premature birth, difficult labour, asphyxia); and after birth (infectious diseases, trauma or shock affecting the child). Convulsions cannot be regarded as causes but only as symptoms of the affection. The aetiological part played by inherited syphilis is recognized as important. There is no exclusive relation between any one of these aetiologies and any one type of cerebral diplegia, but preferential relations are often apparent. The view that cerebral diplegias are affections with a single aetiology is untenable.

The pathological findings in the diplegias are of many kinds, and in general the same as in the hemiplegias; for the most part they are in the nature of end stages, from which it is not invariably possible to infer back to the initial lesions. They do not as a rule allow of a decision as to the aetiological category to which a case is to be referred. Nor is it usually possible to deduce the clinical picture from the postmortem findings; so that the assumption that there are intimate and exclusive relations between clinical types and anatomical changes must also be rejected.

The pathological physiology of cerebral diplegias has an essential connection with the two characteristics by which both general and paraplegic spasticity are distinguished from other manifestations of organic disease of the cerebrum. For in both these clinical forms contracture predominates over paralysis and the lower extremities are affected more severely than the upper ones. The discussion in this paper reaches the conclusion that the more intense affection of the lower extremities in general and paraplegic spasticity must be connected with the localization of the lesion (meningeal haemorrhage along the median fissure) and the preponderance of contracture with the superficiality of the lesion. The strabismus of diplegic children, which is particularly common in paraplegic spasticity and where premature birth is the aetiology, is traceable to the retinal haemorrhages in new-born children described by Königstein.

A special section directs attention to the numerous instances of the familial and hereditary occurrence of children's diseases which show a clinical affinity with cerebral diplegias.

On familial forms of cerebral diplegias.

An observation of two brothers, one six and a half and the other five years old, whose parents were blood relations, and who present a complicated clinical picture which has gradually developed, in the one case since birth and in the other since the second year. The symptoms of this familial disorder (lateral nystagmus, atrophy of the optic nerve, alternating convergent strabismus, monotonous and, as it were, scanning speech, intention tremor of the arms, spastic weakness of the legs, accompanied by high intelligence) give grounds for constructing a new affection which is to be regarded as a spastic counterpart to Friedreich's disease. Emphasis is laid on the far-reaching similarity of these cases to those described as multiple sclerosis by Pelizaeus in 1885.

The cerebral diplegias of children.

A summary of the findings in the monograph abstracted above.

Some points for a comparative study of organic and hysterical motor paralyses.

A comparison between organic and hysterical paralyses made under the influence of Charcot in order to arrive at a line of approach to the nature of hysteria. Organic paralysis is either periphero-spinal or cerebral. On the basis of discussions in my critical study on the aphasias, the former is described as projection paralysis and is paralysis en détail, and the latter is described as representation paralysis and is paralysis en masse. Hysteria imitates only the latter category of paralyses but has freedom to specialize which makes it resemble projection paralysis; it can dissociate the areas of paralysis which regularly occur in cerebral affections. Hysterical paralysis has a tendency to excessive development; it can be extremely in tense and yet strictly confined to a small area, while cortical paralysis regularly increases its extent with an increase in its intensity. Sensibility behaves in a directly contrary manner in the two kinds of paralysis.

The special characteristics of cortical paralysis are determined by the peculiarities of cerebral structure, and allow us to infer back to the anatomy of the brain. Hysterical paralysis on the contrary behaves as though there were no such thing as cerebral anatomy. Hysteria knows nothing of the anatomy of the brain. The alteration which underlies hysterical paralysis can have no resemblance to organic lesions but must be looked for in the conditions governing the accessibility of some particular circle of ideas.

The neuro-psychoses of defense:

An attempt at a psychological theory of acquired hysteria, of many phobias and obsessions and of certain hallucinatory psychoses.

The first of a series of short papers which now follow and which are directed to the task of preparing a general exposition of the neuroses on a new basis which is now in hand.

The splitting of consciousness in hysteria is not a primary characteristic of this neurosis, based on degenerative weakness, as Janet insists. It is the consequence of a peculiar psychical process known as defense which is shown by some short reports of analyses to be present not only in hysteria but in numerous other neuroses and psychoses. Defense comes into operation when an instance of incompatibility arises in ideational life between a particular idea and the ego'. The process of may be figuratively represented as though the quota of excitation were torn away from the idea that is to be repressed and put to some other use.. This can occur in a variety of ways: in hysteria the liberated sum of excitation is transformed into somatic innervation (conversion hysteria); in obsessional neurosis it remains in the psychical field and attaches itself to other ideas which are not incompatible in themselves and which are thus substitutes for the repressed idea. The source of the incompatible ideas which are subjected to defense is solely and exclusively sexual life. An analysis of a case of hallucinatory psychosis shows that this psychosis too represents a method of achieving defense.

Obsessions and phobias:
Their psychical mechanism and aetiology.

Obsessions and phobias are to be distinguished from neurasthenia as independent neurotic affections. In both it is a question of the linkage between an idea and an affective state. In phobias the latter is always the same, namely anxiety; in true obsessions it can be of various kinds (self-reproach, sense of guilt, doubt, etc.). The affective state emerges as the essential element of the obsession, since it remains unaltered in the individual case, whereas the idea attached to it is changed. Psychical analysis shows that the affect of the obsession is justified in every instance, but that the idea attached to it represents a substitute for an idea derived from sexual life which is more appropriate to the affect and which has succumbed to repression. This state of affairs is illustrated by numerous short analyses of cases of folie du doute, washing mania, arithmomania, etc., in which the reinstatement of the repressed idea was successful and accompanied by useful therapeutic effects. The phobias in the strict sense are reserved for the paper on anxiety neurosis.

Made in United States
Orlando, FL
01 May 2022